Countries of the World

Kenya

Bridget Giles

Chege Githiora and Tabitha Otieno, Consultants

NATIONAL GEOGRAPHIC

WASHINGTON, D.C.

Contents

4   Foreword

7   GEOGRAPHY

From Savanna to Snow

8   At a Glance
> What's the Weather Like?
> Fast Facts
> Average Temperature & Rainfall
> Physical Map

11   Special Feature:
Sacred Mountain

12   Special Feature Map:
Rifting Through Kenya

15   NATURE

Wealth of Wildlife

16   At a Glance
> Diverse Ecosystems
> Species at Risk
> Vegetation & Ecosystems Map

18   Special Feature Map:
Masai Mara Migration

20   Special Feature:
Maneless Man-eaters?

24   Special Feature:
Wangari Maathai

27   HISTORY

All Human History

28	At a Glance
	> The First Herders and Farmers
	> Time line
	> Historical Map
31	Special Feature Map: Fossils and their Finders
32	Special Feature Map: Trading Network
34	Special Feature: Dedan Kimathi

37 PEOPLE & CULTURE
Many Cultures and Tongues

38	At a Glance
	> Rural & Urban Population
	> Common Swahili Phrases
	> Population Map
45	Special Feature: Street Talk
46	Special Feature: National Holidays

49 GOVERNMENT & ECONOMY
A New Nation

50	At a Glance
	> Provinces and Presidents
	> Trading Partners
	> Political Map
52	Special Feature: Jomo Kenyatta
53	Special Feature: How the Government Works
56	Special Feature Map: Agriculture

58	Add a Little Extra to Your Country Report!
60	Glossary
61	Bibliography
	Further Information
62	Index
64	Credits

Foreword

P RESENT DAY KENYA is thought to be the home of the earliest species of modern human beings. The country's position between the Indian Ocean and Lake Victoria means that people from all over Africa and the Middle East have traveled and traded across it for centuries. The result is a diverse culture that includes 60 ethnic groups speaking distinct languages and dialects.

Kenyans enjoy a warm equatorial climate throughout the year, with relatively warm lowlands and much cooler highlands. Kenyans are proud hosts to visitors from all over the world who come to share the outdoor experience. Tourism is an important industry that caters to the largest number of adventure travelers in Africa, making Kenya the most famous safari destination in the world.

Like much of Africa and Southeast Asia, Kenya is grappling with AIDS. Many children have been orphaned and the country struggles to provide medical care for the desperately ill. Kenya has begun educating its people about how the disease is transmitted, how to care for its victims, and how to avoid infection. New hope comes from international efforts to make expensive AIDS medicines available to sufferers.

Kenya also faces challenges from political instability and internal conflicts in neighboring countries. Many refugees flee to Kenya to seek shelter from turmoil at home. Kenya is densely populated and refugee problems have intensified its struggle to meet the needs of its own citizens while giving sanctuary to others.

This book gives a panoramic view of Kenya—its geography, environment, history, culture, politics, and economy. The reader will come to understand why Kenya is such a popular destination and why it has

been selected as the headquarters of many world organizations. Although Kenya faces challenges, it remains a haven of political stability on the African continent; and its wildlife, pleasant climate, world-famous scenery, and fascinating cultures continue to attract visitors from all over the world.

▲ **Most Kenyan children see education as their chance of a better future and so they work hard at school.**

T. Otieno

Tabitha Otieno, Ph.D.
Professor of Social Science and
Chair of Cultural and Social Studies
Jackson State University

From
Savanna
to
Snow

EVEN IF YOU have never been to Kenya, you probably know what it looks like. Kenya's savanna is familiar from hundreds of movies, TV programs, books, and commercials. It is the landscape many people imagine when they think of Africa. But nothing will prepare you for the excitement of going out on safari. Everyone is on the alert, trying to be the first to spot a giraffe, a wildebeest, or a lion. Suddenly that distant rock you are scanning through your binoculars flaps its ears and you realize that you are looking at your first elephant. Millions of people visit Kenya in the hope of experiencing that special thrill. Others come to relax on the soft white sands of Kenya's beaches and swim in the warm waters of the Indian Ocean.

◀ **The giraffe's long neck enables it to eat food that no other animal can reach, such as the spiky leaves of this thorn tree.**

WHAT'S THE WEATHER LIKE?

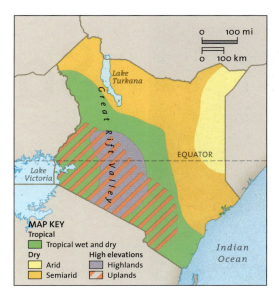

K enya lies within the tropics, a broad band that circles the Earth at its widest point. The climate is warm or hot all year round, and there are only two seasons— rainy and dry. The highlands are the coolest and wettest parts of Kenya. The farther north and east, the longer the dry season and the less the rainfall. Drought is a frequent problem. The map opposite shows the physical features of Kenya. Labels on this map and on similar maps throughout this book identify places pictured in each chapter.

Fast Facts

OFFICIAL NAME: Republic of Kenya

FORM OF GOVERNMENT: republic

CAPITAL: Nairobi

POPULATION: 33,830,000

OFFICIAL LANGUAGES: Swahili and English

MONETARY UNIT: Kenyan shilling

AREA: 224,081 square miles (580,367 square kilometers)

BORDERING NATIONS: Tanzania, Uganda, Sudan, Ethiopia, and Somalia

HIGHEST POINT: Mount Kenya 17,058 feet (5,199 m)

LOWEST POINT: Indian Ocean 0 feet (0 meters)

MAJOR MOUNTAIN RANGES: Aberdare Range, Mau Escarpment

MAJOR RIVERS: Athi/Galana and Tana

Average Temperature & Rainfall

Average High/Low Temperatures; Yearly Rainfall

Mombasa (Coast):
89° F (32° C)/68° F (20° C); 45 in (114 cm)
Nairobi (Central Highlands):
78° F (26° C)/69° F (21° C); 29 in (76 cm)
Kisumu (Western Plateau):
85° F (30° C)/62° F (17° C); 45 in (115 cm)
Amboseli National Park (Southern Plains):
91° F (33° C)/82° F (28° C); 12 in (30 cm)
Moyale (Northern Plains):
80° F (27° C)/64° F (18° C); 27 in (70 cm)

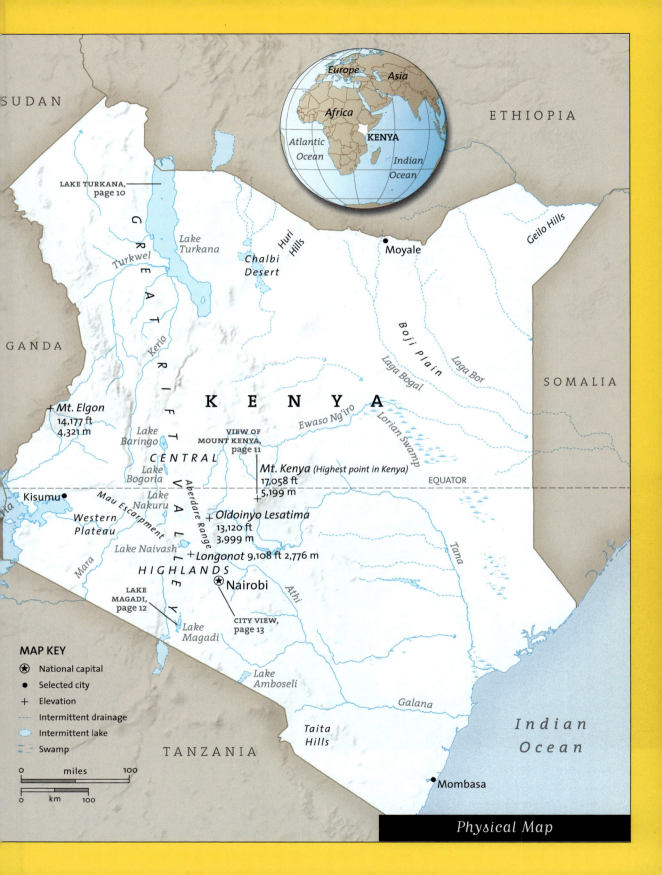

SUDAN

ETHIOPIA

Europe   Asia

Africa   **KENYA**

Atlantic   Indian
Ocean   Ocean

LAKE TURKANA,
page 10

*Lake
Turkana*

Turkwel

G R E A T

Kerio

GANDA

R I F T

+ *Mt. Elgon*
14,177 ft
4,321 m

*Lake
Baringo*

C E N T R A L

*Lake
Bogoria*

Kisumu •

*Lake
Nakuru*

Mau Escarpment

*Western
Plateau*

V A L L E Y

Aberdare Range

Lake Naivash

H I G H L A N D S

LAKE
MAGADI,
page 12

*Lake
Magadi*

Mara

TANZANIA

*Huri
Hills*

*Chalbi
Desert*

• *Moyale*

Geilo Hills

B o j i   P l a i n

Laga Bogal

Laga Bor

SOMALIA

K E N Y A

Ewaso Ng'iro

Lorian Swamp

VIEW OF
MOUNT KENYA,
page 11

Mt. Kenya (Highest point in Kenya)
17,058 ft
5,199 m

EQUATOR

+ *Oldoinyo Lesatima*
13,120 ft
3,999 m

+ *Longonot* 9,108 ft 2,776 m

⊛ *Nairobi*

CITY VIEW,
page 13

Athi

Tana

*Lake
Amboseli*

Galana

*Taita
Hills*

*I n d i a n
O c e a n*

MAP KEY

⊛ National capital
• Selected city
+ Elevation
- - - Intermittent drainage
▨ Intermittent lake
▨ Swamp

0 ——————— 100
    miles

0 ——————— 100
    km

• *Mombasa*

Physical Map

The Fertile Highlands

Nearly all of southwestern Kenya is cool, wet highland. The days there are sunny and pleasant. The altitude makes the climate near-perfect for growing crops or raising livestock.

White clouds drift across the landscape, creating a changing pattern of light and shadow. At night, the temperature falls sharply, and herders cluster around log fires.

Millions of years ago volcanoes erupted in this region. The ash they scattered created a rich, fertile soil that is ideal for growing crops of all kinds, from coffee and flowers to vegetables.

There are two rainy seasons, known as the "long rains," from about March to May, and the "short rains," from about October to December. If the long rains fail to arrive, farmers and herders prepare for drought and anxiously watch the skies in the last months of the year.

▼ A cinder cone rises dramatically from the jade-green water of Lake Turkana. Cinder cones are created when a deposit of cinders builds up around a volcanic vent, gradually forming a conical hill with a bowl-shaped crater.

The Plains

Dry grassy plains with scattered hills cover much of central Kenya. In the southeast, the plains become the savannas so

SACRED MOUNTAIN

The jagged peak of Mount Kenya thrusts 17,058 feet (5,199 m) into a brilliant blue tropical sky. It is the highest mountain in the country and the second highest in Africa. Millions of years ago this volcano belched fire and smoke; today it is capped by snow and has small glaciers, or slow-moving rivers of ice. The top of the mountain is so high and so cold that the snow and ice never melt, even at the height of Kenya's dry season.

The Gikuyu people believed that the mountain was home to their god, Ngai. They called it Kirinyaga, meaning Mountain of Beauty. Former British rulers, who could not say the Gikuyu name correctly, named the peak and the country Kenya.

▲ When early explorers reported a snow-capped mountain near the Equator, no one believed them.

popular with tourists. To the north and northeast, the plains become drier and more desertlike. The rainy season gets shorter. Months go by with no rain. It finally falls hard and fast, filling up dry riverbeds and turning roads into raging creeks.

Coastal Lowlands

In the east, the savannas and plains merge with the coastal lowlands on the Indian Ocean. Well-watered by rivers, streams, and the regular seasonal rains, the

RIFTING THROUGH KENYA

One of the most stunning natural wonders of the world passes through Kenya—the Great Rift Valley, a gigantic tear in the Earth's crust that has been forming for 30 million years. The Rift stretches 4,000 miles (6,400 km) from the Middle East to southern Africa. As the Central Rift, it passes through Kenya from north to south. The valley averages 30 to 40 miles (48 to 64 km) wide. On either side, the land rises steeply to heights of up to 9,000 feet (2,700 m). The Rift lies along a fault between the giant plates that make up the Earth's surface, and there is lots of geological activity there. Most of the Rift's volcanoes, such as mounts Elgon and Kenya, are inactive, but many hot springs and geysers erupt from the valley floor. All of Kenya's lakes lie within the Rift Valley.

▼ The bed of Lake Magadi is almost solid soda (sodium carbonate). As underground water passes through the bedrock it turns a bright pink.

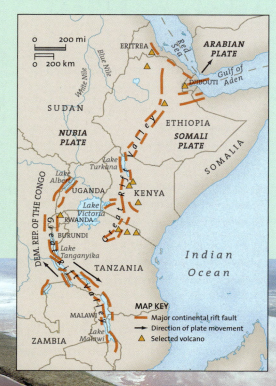

MAP KEY

— Major continental rift fault

→ Direction of plate movement

▲ Selected volcano

soil is fertile and good for crops. Beaches with white coral sand, shaded by palm and coconut trees, line the coast. Around river mouths, the tangled roots of mangrove trees hold the swampy land together, preventing it from washing into the sea. Coral reefs with their varied and colorful sea life attract snorklers and divers.

Contrasting Cities

Nairobi, Kenya's bustling capital, is just under 6,000 feet (1,820 m) above sea level. People who aren't used to being so high above sea level take a few days to get used to the thin air. Only five miles (8 km) south of the city lions roam in one of Kenya's many national parks. Nairobi is a modern city, but cities near the coast have existed for longer. Mombasa's maze of narrow streets is full of architecture that shows the long influence of the Arabs who began living there in the 700s. Everyone learns to move slowly in the steamy heat.

▲ A diver spots a lion-fish as she explores the magical underwater world of the coral reefs.

▼ Founded in 1899 as a railway camp Nairobi is now one of Africa's largest cities.

Wealth
of
Wildlife

FOR PEOPLE WHO like wildlife, Kenya is one of the most exciting countries in the world. Nearly every species of large land mammal lives there. There are hunters like lions and cheetahs, and peaceful herbivores like elephants and giraffes. Hippos live near the creeks and water holes. In the trees are scores of monkeys. Hundreds of types of antelope graze the varied habitats. There are shy forest dwellers like the bongo, which is hard to spot, and other antelopes like wildebeests that cross the grasslands in huge herds. In the past, many Europeans and Americans went on hunting trips, called safaris, to shoot animals for sport. The Kenyans banned hunting in the 1970s. Today millions of visitors still go on safari—but the only legal shooting is with a camera.

◀ **A rainbow provides a dramatic backdrop for impala, gazelles, and giraffes in Lake Nakuru National Park.**

At a Glance

DIVERSE ECOSYSTEMS

The map opposite shows Kenya's main vegetation zones—or what grows where. Vegetation zones form ecosystems. Kenya's varied ecosystems include deserts, semideserts, savannas, coastal swamps, and forests. Each has its own mix of plants and animals that are ideally suited to those particular conditions. Elephants, however, have to feed for at least 14 hours a day to fuel their huge bodies, so they live anywhere they can find enough food. Lions live in both forests and savannas. The forest-dwelling lions have more spots than their cousins on the plains. In the dappled light among the trees, the spots help conceal, or camouflage, the lions when they hunt their prey.

► Scientists think that the striking chestnut and white coloration of bongos may help the animals identify one another in the dense rain forest.

Species at Risk

There are more than 30 endangered species in Kenya. Seven are classed as critically endangered, because there is a high risk that they may soon become extinct. Although elephants, lions, and cheetahs are not endangered they are classed as vulnerable, because they are threatened by the loss of their natural homes, conflict with people, and by illegal hunting. The African wild dog is also threatened by diseases caught from domestic dogs. The following are some of Kenya's endangered species:

> Aberdare cisticola (bird)
> Aders' duiker (antelope)
> African wild dog
> Amani sunbird
> Basra reed warbler
> Black rhino
> Bongo (antelope)
> Clarke's weaverbird
> Du Toit's torrent frog
> Green turtle
> Giant thicket rat
> Giant wrasse (fish)

> Grevy's zebra
> Hirola (antelope)
> Sharpe's longclaw (bird)
> Sokoke pipit (bird)
> Sokoke Scops owl
> Spotted ground, or forest, thrush
> Taita apalis (bird)
> Taita thrush
> Taita white-eye (bird)
> Tana colobus monkey
> Turner's eremomela (bird)

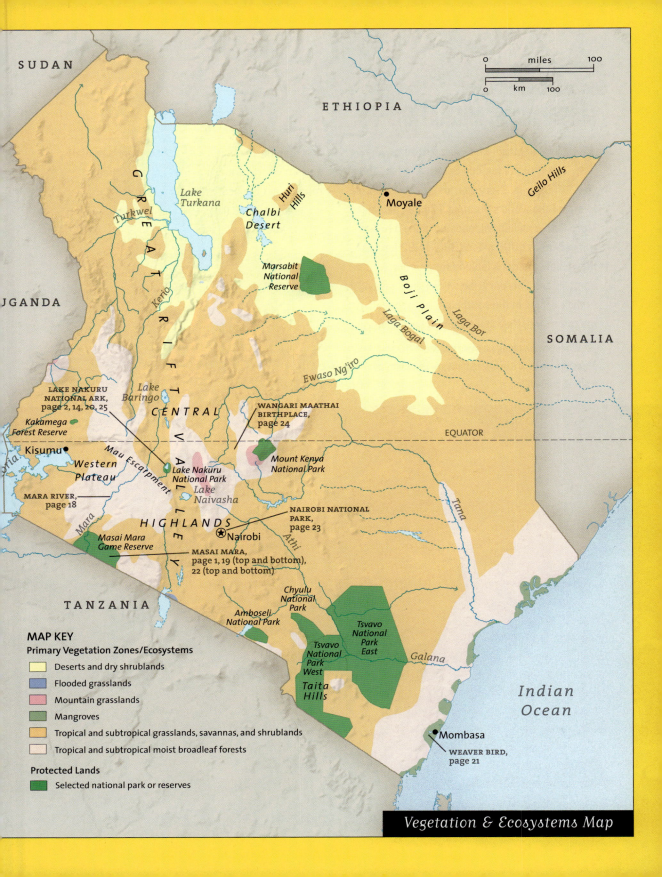

SUDAN

ETHIOPIA

UGANDA

SOMALIA

TANZANIA

Lake Turkana

Turkwel

Kerio

G R E A T   R I F T

Huri Hills

Chalbi Desert

● Moyale

Gello Hills

Marsabit National Reserve

Boji Plain

Laga Bogal

Laga Bor

Ewaso Ng'iro

LAKE NAKURU NATIONAL ARK, page 2, 14, 20, 25

Kakamega Forest Reserve

Lake Baringo

C E N T R A L

V A L L E Y

WANGARI MAATHAI BIRTHPLACE, page 24

EQUATOR

● Kisumu

Western Plateau

Mau Escarpment

Lake Nakuru National Park

Lake Naivasha

Mount Kenya National Park

MARA RIVER, page 18

Mara

H I G H L A N D S

⍟ Nairobi

Masai Mara Game Reserve

Athi

NAIROBI NATIONAL PARK, page 23

MASAI MARA, page 1, 19 (top and bottom), 22 (top and bottom)

Tana

Chyulu National Park

Amboseli National Park

Tsvavo National Park West

Tsvavo National Park East

Galana

Taita Hills

Indian Ocean

● Mombasa

WEAVER BIRD, page 21

MAP KEY
Primary Vegetation Zones/Ecosystems

- Deserts and dry shrublands
- Flooded grasslands
- Mountain grasslands
- Mangroves
- Tropical and subtropical grasslands, savannas, and shrublands
- Tropical and subtropical moist broadleaf forests

Protected Lands

- Selected national park or reserves

miles 100

km 100

Vegetation & Ecosystems Map

MASAI MARA MIGRATION

Kenya's Masai Mara game reserve is next to the famous Serengeti Plain of Tanzania. Every year the reserve is home to one of the world's greatest wildlife spectacles. More than a million wildebeests make a round trip of 500 to 1,000 miles (800–1,600 km) as they follow the rains looking for pasture. In January and February, the wildebeests give birth to their calves in the southeastern Serengeti. As the rains stop, they move west to Lake Victoria,

▼ **Wildebeests plunge across the Mara River. Many drown or are dragged beneath the water by waiting crocodiles.**

and then north into the Mara. Each year's rainfall pattern varies, and the animals change their route to get the best grass. They can tell if it is raining over 30 miles (50 km) away, but no one knows how.

Lake Victoria

KENYA

Mara

Jul – Oct

MASAI MARA GAME RESERVE

0   mi   50

0   km   50

May – June   SERENGETI NATIONAL PARK

Lake Natron

Serengeti Plain

TANZANIA

Nov – April
NGORONGORO CONSERVATION AREA

MASWA GAME RESERVE

+ Ngorongoro Crater

MAP KEY
— Protected area
▢ Wildebeest concentration
→ Wildebeest migration flow

Lake Eyasi

Lake Manyara

Savanna Herds and Hunters

The grasslands are a dangerous place. They have many hunters and few places to hide. The animals that live there have to be large and powerful, like elephants and rhinos. Or they need to be like zebras and antelopes, which are fast and have sharp senses that warn them of danger.

Zebras, giraffes, and antelopes feed on the tough grasses and scattered trees of the savannas. The greenery springs up after seasonal rains, so the herds move across the plains to find food. In turn they are shadowed by carnivores—lions, cheetahs, African wild dogs, hyenas, and jackals.

Because the savanna is so dangerous, the babies of many animals can stand up within minutes of being born. They are ready to flee from danger. A baby giraffe can run with its herd when it is only two or three days old. Its mother defends her calf from predators by swinging her head like a battering ram or kicking with her long legs.

▲ The zebra's stripes may act as camouflage at dawn and dusk when many predators hunt.

▼ Lions are sociable animals, forming groups called prides.

MANELESS MAN-EATERS?

The lions from Tsavo (SAH-vo) in southeastern Kenya have a fearsome reputation as man-eaters. In 1898 workers building a bridge on the Mombasa–Uganda railroad were terrorized for months by a pair of lions. The animals killed more than 130 men before they were finally shot. But the Tsavo lions may not fully deserve their reputation. They probably do attack people more often than their southern cousins in the Serengeti, but that is because Tsavo lions often live nearer to people and in a tougher environment, where water and food are more scarce. Whether or not they are man-eaters, Tsavo lions are unique. The males have no mane; a maned male would overheat in the hot, dry climate. Unusually, males also live in bachelor (male-only) groups until ready to rule a pride alone.

▼ The black rhino has very poor eyesight but a keen sense of smell and hearing. If taken by surprise it is likely to charge the intruder.

Most times she can fight off an attack, but even so only about half of the baby giraffes will survive their first year.

A lion cub, on the other hand, has few enemies. It does not need to grow up so quickly. It lives on milk from the females in its pride for about six months. While the adults laze in the shade, the cubs have play fights. Their games teach them the skills they need to begin hunting when they are four or five months old. Whatever the pride kills, the cubs are allowed to eat only when the adults have had enough.

Life in the Highlands

Kenya's highlands are home to many animals that live nowhere else. The patches of forest in the Taita Hills are home to three of Kenya's endangered birds—the Taita apalis, Taita thrush, and the Taita white-eye. In fact, nine of Kenya's endangered species are birds of the highland forests. The needs of wildlife and the needs of people have come into conflict in many of Kenya's forest areas. People have cut down trees for firewood or to clear land for farming. Animals that live in the forests find it hard to survive. The shy mountain bongo with its glossy, white-and-chestnut-striped coat has almost vanished. In 2004 conservationists brought 18 bongos to Kenya from zoos in the United States. They

▼ The male weaver-bird makes a grass nest with an entrance at the bottom. He attracts females by calling and fluttering his wings.

planned to breed captive bongos and release them into the wild. So far several calves have been born and three males are about to be released.

Kakamega Forest in western Kenya is a patch of tropical rain

▲ Cheetah cubs stay with their mother for about a year before they can hunt successfully on their own.

▼ Disputes between male hippos begin with yawns that show off their huge teeth.

forest. More kinds of plants and animals live in rain forests than in any other habitat. Kakamega is home to more than 300 species of birds, 350 species of trees, 27 species of snakes, and 400 species of butterflies. High in the trees are colobus monkeys with black fur fringed with white. Their long fur has a special purpose. As the monkeys make great leaps of up to 20 feet (6 m) from tree to tree, the fur fans out. It forms a parachute, so they do not fall too quickly.

The mountainsides are covered in other types of vegetation, including evergreen forests and forests of bamboo. Higher up, the soil is too rocky for trees. The ground is covered in tufts of grass and giant lobelias, which look like a cross between a cactus and a pineapple. The flowers of the groundsel tree look like cabbages—but they are not so good to eat.

Looking After Nature

The Kenyans are proud of their rich wildlife. They have created more than 50 national parks and reserves to protect every type of ecosystem in the country. The most famous are Tsavo East, Tsavo West, Amboseli, and the Masai Mara, in the savannas. Visitors can go to other parks to see life in the forests and highlands. From the capital, Nairobi, visitors often head to Mzima Springs in Tsavo National Park. The pools have underwater viewing tanks where visitors can watch hippos. The animals look slow and clumsy on land, but in the water they are graceful and quick swimmers.

Lake Nakuru National Park is a bird-watchers' paradise. Hundreds of thousands of flamingos feed on the algae that forms on the lake bed. When they take to the air, they fill the brilliant blue sky with a huge pink cloud. It is one of nature's great spectacles.

▼ A vervet monkey and her young in Nairobi National Park. The baby spends its first week of life clinging to its mother.

WANGARI MAATHAI

Wangari Maathai was born in Nyeri in 1940. She was the first woman in central or eastern Africa to earn a doctorate (Ph.D.) and the first female head of a university department in Kenya. In 1977 she set up the Green Belt Movement (GBM) to work with ordinary people and especially women to improve the environment and to empower people and communities. Women of the GBM have planted 30 million trees on farms, schools,

and church compounds. Maathai campaigned against developers grabbing forest land; she was arrested and imprisoned. An international letter-writing campaign helped free her. In 2002 she was elected to parliament. In 2004 she became the first African woman to be awarded the Nobel Peace Prize.

Along the coast, marine parks protect the coral reefs, mangrove swamps, and sea-grass meadows.

Every year the population of Kenya grows. More wild animals come into conflict with herders, farmers, or hunters. People kill elephants for their valuable ivory tusks, antelope for meat, and lions because they kill people and

livestock. The Kenyan Wildlife Service (KWS) asks local people to help them manage wildlife. The KWS builds fences, pays farmers whose crops are damaged, and explains how protecting wildlife can benefit communities by bringing money to the area.

▲ The pink coloring of flamingos' feathers comes from the food they eat, which contains a red pigment.

◄ Jackson's chameleons live only in Kenya and Tanzania. Chameleons are famous for being able to change the color and pattern of their skin.

All Human History

IMAGINE TRYING to spot a piece of black bone the size of a matchbook in jumbled volcanic rock. You'd need super eyes! But that's just what Kamoya Kimeu did one day in 1984 in Kenya's Turkana Basin. He found a small piece of skull. Over the next five years a team of scientists found and put together the rest of the skeleton. It belonged to an apelike human, or hominid, who lived 1.5 million years ago. The bones were so old they had turned to rocks, called fossils. The team had found one of our earliest ancestors.

Fossil hunters have made many finds in Kenya. The fossils show that hominids changed over millions of years. Most scientists believe that they developed into modern humans. Northern Kenya and nearby Tanzania may have been the origin of everyone on the Earth.

◄ **Famed fossil hunter, Kamoya Kimeu, searches for new finds on the barren, rocky ground near Lake Turkana.**

THE FIRST HERDERS AND FARMERS

One of the best ways to understand prehistory, the time before people learned how to write, is by studying where people live who speak different languages. There are three main groups of related languages in Kenya: Cushitic, Nilotic, and Bantu. The map opposite shows where these early peoples came from and where they settled. Cushitic herders from the Ethiopian Highlands migrated south. Over centuries they spread as far as central Tanzania. Nilotic herders migrated from the Nile River region of southern Sudan, settling first in the high

▲ Ariaal boys herd cattle in the far north of Kenya. The Ariaal are Cushitic herders who lead a nomadic life, moving with their animals to fresh pastures.

northern plateau of Kenya, then in the plains, and finally near Lake Victoria. Meanwhile, over several thousand years, Bantu speakers spread out from their homeland somewhere in the forests between the Niger and Congo rivers of west-central Africa. By 500 B.C. they had begun to arrive in the East African savannas, reaching the Kenyan coast several hundred years later. Bantu speakers introduced the use of iron tools.

Time line

This chart shows the approximate dates for the peopling of Kenya from the arrival of early herders to Arab and European traders and settlers. The early migrations took place over thousands of years.

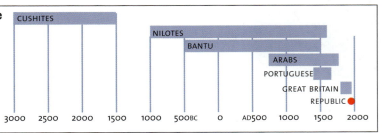

CUSHITES

NILOTES

BANTU

ARABS

PORTUGUESE

GREAT BRITAIN

REPUBLIC

3000 2500 2000 1500 1000 500BC 0 AD500 1000 1500 2000

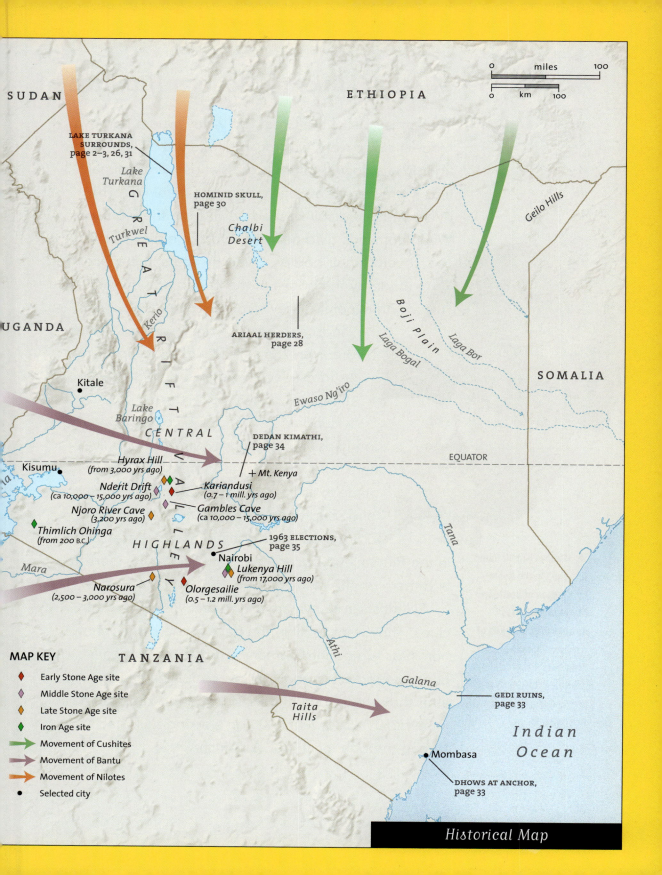

SUDAN

LAKE TURKANA
SURROUNDS,
page 2–3, 26, 31

*Lake
Turkana*

Turkwel

Kerio

ETHIOPIA

HOMINID SKULL,
page 30

*Chalbi
Desert*

Geilo Hills

ARIAAL HERDERS,
page 28

Boji Plain

Laga Bor

Laga Bogal

SOMALIA

UGANDA

Kitale

*Lake
Baringo*

CENTRAL

Ewaso Ng'iro

EQUATOR

DEDAN KIMATHI,
page 34

Kisumu

Hyrax Hill
(from 3,000 yrs ago)

+ Mt. Kenya

Nderit Drift
(ca 10,000 – 15,000 yrs ago)

Karianusi
(0.7 – 1 mill. yrs ago)

Njoro River Cave
(3,200 yrs ago)

Gambles Cave
(ca 10,000 – 15,000 yrs ago)

Thimlich Ohinga
(from 200 B.C.)

Tana

HIGHLANDS

1963 ELECTIONS,
page 35

Mara

Nairobi

Lukenya Hill
(from 17,000 yrs ago)

Narosura
(2,500 – 3,000 yrs ago)

Olorgesailie
(0.5 – 1.2 mill. yrs ago)

MAP KEY

◆ Early Stone Age site
◆ Middle Stone Age site
◆ Late Stone Age site
◆ Iron Age site
→ Movement of Cushites
→ Movement of Bantu
→ Movement of Nilotes
● Selected city

TANZANIA

Athi

Galana

GEDI RUINS,
page 33

*Taita
Hills*

*Indian
Ocean*

● Mombasa

DHOWS AT ANCHOR,
page 33

Historical Map

Missing Links to Modern Humans

The landscape of the Great Rift Valley, where Kamoya made his discovery, was much different a million years ago. Rivers flowed through grasslands full of animal life. There was plenty of food for the hominids. The rivers deposited soil washed down from the highlands. When hominids died near the rivers, the new soil covered their bodies. Over the years, the spaces made by the bones of the buried hominids filled with minerals. They formed stone fossils. When the landscape became drier, wind and water wore away the soil. The fossils reappeared on the surface, where you can still pick them up today.

Hundreds of thousands of years after hominids lived in Kenya, early humans lived there. They had learned to make tools. They made axes from sharp pieces of hard rock, and used them to cut up animals for food. Today, thousands of hand axes are scattered in the Rift Valley—but you need to be a real expert to find them on the stony ground.

Scientists in Kenya are like detectives looking for clues. They want to fill in the gaps in the story of how hominids turned into humans. They know that early humans used stone tools for over a million years, even after they stopped hunting and began to keep animals in herds. By about A.D. 500 iron working skills had spread through much of East Africa.

▲ Kamoya Kimeu found this skull in the Koobi Fora region of northern Kenya in 1973. It is smaller than the skull of a modern human and so scientists disagree about whether it belonged to a prehuman species or to a hominid.

FOSSILS AND THEIR FINDERS

East Africa's most famous fossil hunters are often called the Hominid Gang. Louis and Mary Leakey began their research in the 1930s at Olduvai Gorge in Tanzania, where they made the first of their startling discoveries. In 1959 Mary found a hominid fossil from about 1.7 million years ago. It seemed to indicate that humans began in Africa, not Asia as scientists then believed.

Their son Richard intended to follow a different career but he became hooked on fossil-hunting when he found a near-human jaw in 1963. In 1972 he and Bernard Ngeneo discovered a hominid skull, dating from 1.9 million years ago.

▼ Maeve and Richard Leakey and their team examine fossil finds in northern Kenya.

It is the oldest *Homo habilis* skull found so far. *Homo habilis* is one of the earliest species of modern human.

Richard's wife Maeve and their daughter Louise have followed in the Leakey tradition and both of them have led fossil-finding expeditions in northern Kenya.

Kamoya Kimeu and Bernard Ngeneo are key members of the Leakey team and have been responsible for making some of the most important fossil discoveries.

TRADING NETWORK

The East African coast and islands had many natural harbors. From the first century A.D. Phoenician, Roman, Greek, and Indian sailors traded with local Africans and founded settlements. They were followed by Arabs starting in the 700s. The Arabs had developed a triangular sail that made their boats, called dhows, more efficient than the square-sailed European boats. They soon dominated the coastal trade and settled in the ports. Trading routes linked the prosperous settlements with inland centers.

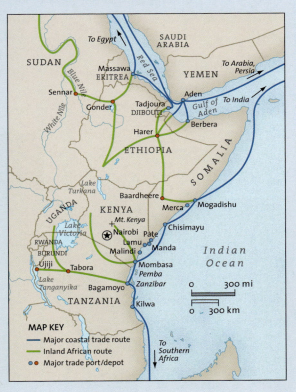

MAP KEY
— Major coastal trade route
— Inland African route
•• Major trade port/depot

Ancient Traders

Nearly 2,000 years ago a Greek merchant wrote one of the world's first guidebooks. It was a little like the travel books people take on vacation today. It told traders how to get from place to place, and what they could buy and sell. The book described how ships visited East Africa from India, on the other side of the Indian Ocean.

Indians were not the only visitors to East Africa. Many different peoples mixed with the Bantu speakers who lived near the coast. They created the modern-day Swahili people. Their name means "of the coast" in the Arabic language.

Some Swahili merchants became very wealthy, especially during the 1400s. They built stone houses from blocks of dead coral taken from the ocean. They dressed in silk from India, and ate off porcelain brought all the way from China.

Coastal islands and ports like Manda and Pate became rich city-states. Each had its own ruling family, officials, and soldiers. The power of the city-states rose and fell. After centuries, Mombasa and Malindi became the richest ports. Their wealth attracted Portuguese and Turkish sailors. These pirates tried to control trade by attacking towns or forcing them to pay taxes. The Portuguese took over Mombasa. In 1698 Arabs from Oman helped the city of Pate drive out the Portuguese. In the 1800s the Omani Arabs built a powerful empire along the East African coast.

▲ Sailing dhows still anchor in Mombasa's harbor as they have for centuries.

▼ The ruins of Gedi, near Malindi, date from the 12th to 15th century.

A Cruel Trade

Life was dangerous for some Africans under Arab rule. Arab traders captured East Africans and sold them as slaves. Africans also joined in the rich trade. People wanted slaves throughout the Arab empire. In the 1700s European countries such as France, Britain, and Holland also needed slaves

Many Cultures and Tongues

MAGINE BEING in a café where everyone spoke a different language. It would be very exciting, but it might be confusing! It could happen in Kenya. Kenyans speak more than 60 languages and dialects. Almost everyone speaks more than one African language, to make sure they can communicate widely. They also speak Swahili and English, which are used for business and for government.

Kenya's 40 or so ethnic groups share some traditions of music, dance, art, and ways of life. Gikuyu are likely to be farmers, for example, while Masai and Samburu are likely to be animal herders. As people move to the cities, however, they leave their traditional ways of life behind. Kenya's city dwellers have created a vibrant culture drawn from many ethnic groups.

◄ **The shapes, patterns, and colors of the beaded jewelry worn by a Masai woman indicate her age and whether she has given birth to a son.**

RURAL & URBAN POPULATION

The map opposite shows that most of Kenya's more than 30 million people live in the highlands and along the southeast coast. Before the 1900s very few people lived in towns and cities. Nairobi did not exist until the 1890s, but today more than 3 million people live there. During the colonial era, life in rural areas became harder as farmers lost their land to white settlers and herders lost their rights to roam with their animals. People began moving to towns and cities in search of jobs. This trend has continued at an increasing pace since independence. In 1955 about 6 percent of Kenyans lived in urban areas; today, nearly 50 percent do.

Common Swahili Phrases

Swahili is Kenya's national language. It is also one of its two official languages; the other is English. Here are some common Swahili words and phrases you might hear in Kenya:

Jambo (JAM-boh) Hello or Good day
U hali gani (oo HAH-lee gah-NEE) How are you?
Ndiyo (DEH-yoo) Yes
Hapana (HAH-pah-nah) No
Tafadhali (THAH-fad-hah-lee) Please
Ahsante (ah-SAHN-teh) Thank you
Hakuna matata (HAH-koo-nah mah-TAH-tah)
   No problems, no worries

▲ Children are often expected to help their parents work on the family farm.

1955 / 7 million	1975 / 13 million	1995 / 27 million	2005 / 34 million
6% Urban / 94% Rural	13% Urban / 87% Rural	30% Urban / 70% Rural	42% Urban / 58% Rural

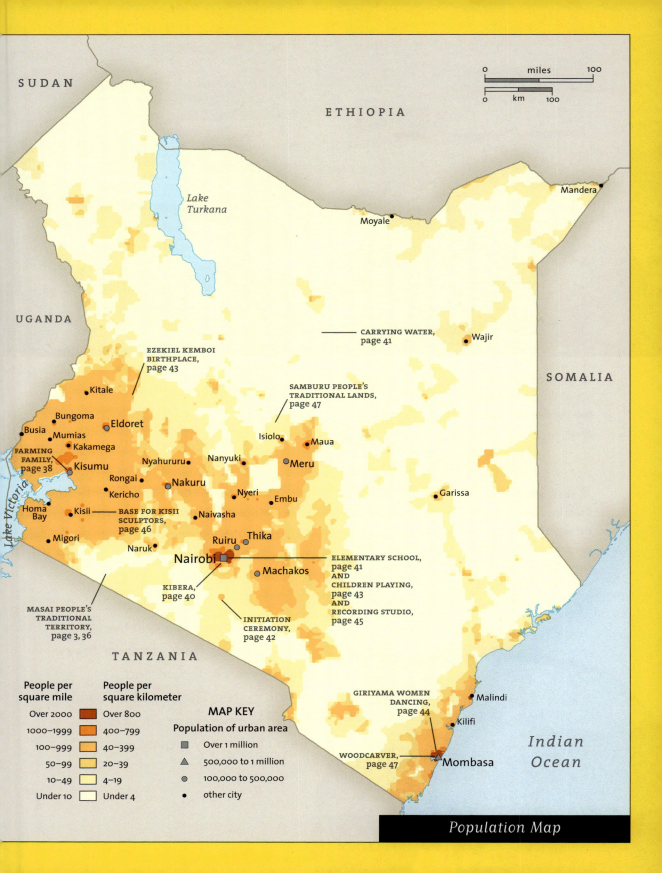

SUDAN

ETHIOPIA

0   miles   100

0   km   100

Mandera

Lake Turkana

Moyale

UGANDA

CARRYING WATER, page 41

Wajir

EZEKIEL KEMBOI BIRTHPLACE, page 43

SAMBURU PEOPLE'S TRADITIONAL LANDS, page 47

SOMALIA

Kitale

Bungoma

Eldoret

Busia

Mumias

Kakamega

FARMING FAMILY, page 38

Kisumu

Isiolo

Maua

Nyahururu

Nanyuki

Meru

Lake Victoria

Rongai

Nakuru

Kericho

Nyeri

Embu

Homa Bay

Kisii

BASE FOR KISII SCULPTORS, page 46

Naivasha

Garissa

Migori

Naruk

Ruiru

Thika

Nairobi

Machakos

ELEMENTARY SCHOOL, page 41 AND CHILDREN PLAYING, page 43 AND RECORDING STUDIO, page 45

KIBERA, page 40

MASAI PEOPLE'S TRADITIONAL TERRITORY, page 3, 36

INITIATION CEREMONY, page 42

TANZANIA

GIRIYAMA WOMEN DANCING, page 44

Malindi

Kilifi

Indian Ocean

WOODCARVER, page 47

Mombasa

People per square mile		People per square kilometer
Over 2000		Over 800
1000–1999		400–799
100–999		40–399
50–99		20–39
10–49		4–19
Under 10		Under 4

MAP KEY
Population of urban area

■   Over 1 million

▲   500,000 to 1 million

●   100,000 to 500,000

•   other city

Population Map

▲ Kibera residents walk to work along the railroad line. The shantytown has no roads.

▼ The Rendile people live in the desert lands of the north. They move camp regularly, so their homes are built like tents that can be folded up and carried away with them.

A City Outside a City

There is not enough good agricultural land to support Kenya's growing population, so people move to cities and towns to look for jobs. Many town dwellers are poor, but they manage to get by as best as they can. Just outside Nairobi lies Africa's poorest and biggest slum, or shantytown: Kibera. Although it only measures about one square mile (2.5 sq km), Kibera is home to close to 1 million people. There are no facilities such as running water, sewers, or electricity. The people of Kibera are creative. They build houses from whatever they can find—even cardboard and packing crates. They run their own small businesses or set up self-help community groups.

Children and the Family

In the country, communities are close. Everyone knows each other, so there are always children to play with or adults to help with chores. Families are large, and grandparents, aunts, uncles, and cousins usually live nearby. Each person has a job to do in the home and the community.

Children in Kenya start elementary school at age six. If there is no school in an area, or not enough desks or books, people get together to build a school or to raise money. School is free, but many children are too busy to go to classes. They help their families working the land, tending cattle, cooking, or fetching water. Even children who do go to school help with many chores, or do jobs to earn extra money. Young girls sometimes walk miles every day to get water.

One of the most important times for Kenyan teenagers is coming of age,

▲ Although this elementary school has no desks the children are eager to learn.

▼ Girls are expected to help their mothers collect water for the family's daily needs.

when they become adults. They often have a special ceremony called initiation. A group of boys or girls of the same age may spend days or weeks living away from home. They learn the skills they will need for their adult lives, how to behave well, and the history and legends of their community. At the end of their initiation, young Masai men dance and sing for four days at the Eunoto festival. In urban areas, however, initiation is getting less and less common.

Just under 45 percent of Kenya's population is below 15 years of age, so although Kenya has seven universities thousands of young Kenyans head to the United States, Europe, and Asia to study.

▲ Young Masai men braid each other's hair and color it with red ocher before an initiation ceremony. As senior warriors they will be allowed to marry and have children.

Play and Sport

Kenyan children love to play. If they don't have any toys, they often make their own from bent wire, beaded jewelry, or old boxes. They play games that do not need much equipment, like *mancala*. It only needs some seeds or stones and a few holes in the ground. Children everywhere play soccer. If they don't have a ball, they kick around a bundle of rags.

Along with soccer, Kenyans enjoy cricket, golf, and boxing. But the sport for which Kenyans are most famous is running. They are experts at long-distance races, such as the marathon. They have set world records and won Olympic gold medals.

▲ Elementary school boys concentrate hard on their hula hoops.

◄ Ezekiel Kemboi celebrates winning the 3,000-meter steeplechase at the 2004 Olympic Games.

▲ Giriyama women
perform a traditional
dance for tourists.

Making Music, Song, and Dance

Every ethnic group in Kenya has its own musical
traditions. While styles are always changing, most
music is based on drums and drumming, so it is great
for dancing. Lively Swahili *taarab* bands combine the
sounds of Africa, Arabia, and India. That makes them
very popular at weddings, where everyone wants to
celebrate. Their songs sometimes poke fun at the
bride and groom and their guests. Since the 1970s
Kenya has also had its own pop music. It uses reggae,
rap, and Cuban rhythms to create a unique style
known as *benga*.

STREET TALK

▲ Emmanuel Jal, a former child soldier and refugee, records a rap song in a Nairobi studio.

Since the 1970s young people living in Nairobi have been creating a language of their own. Sheng was born on the streets as multiethnic groups of friends invented words and mixed and mingled their languages, especially Swahili, English, Gikuyu, Luo, and Kamba. Speaking Sheng gets you a better deal in the market, where it is the language of traders and workers. The champions and geniuses of Sheng are rap and hip-hop artists, and the young men who work on privately owned buses called matatus. At first Sheng was dismissed as a form of slang. Teachers worried that young people would stop learning proper Swahili, and parents wanted to know what their children were saying ! Today, however, nearly every Kenyan city and town has its own version of Sheng. Sheng has even been spoken in parliament.

Telling Stories

Something all Kenyans enjoy is listening to stories. The stories aren't always just for fun. Storytellers pass on the history of the community to young people, and teach them about their own ethnic group. Kenyans have used stories and poems to pass on their beliefs, history, and customs for many centuries. Today, listeners might also learn about health or education from a storyteller or a street theater group.

Many Kenyans enjoy reading. Kenya is proud of its high literacy rate—about 95 percent of people under 24 years of age can read. Swahili people began to

NATIONAL HOLIDAYS

Kenya has 10 official holidays and several important festivals. (Moi Day, the anniversary of the day Daniel arap Moi became president, has been much debated recently and may be dropped).

The dates of Eid al-Fitr change every year because Muslim festivals follow the phases of the moon. This three-day festival takes place at the end of the month-long fast of Ramadan. The Mombasa Carnival with floats and costumes from around the world, is held in November.

JANUARY 1	New Year's Day
MARCH–APRIL	Good Friday
	Easter Monday
MAY 1	Labor Day (International Workers' Day)
JUNE 1	Madaraka (Self-rule) Day
OCTOBER 10	Moi Day
OCTOBER 20	Kenyatta Day
DECEMBER 12	Jamhuri Day (Independence Day)
DECEMBER 25	Christmas Day
DECEMBER 26	Boxing Day

► Skilled Kisii sculptors carve works from soapstone mined in western Kenya.

write poetry more than 300 years ago. Since the early 1900s, Kenyans have been writing books in English, Swahili, and other African languages. Some writers, such as Ngugi wa Thiong'o and Rebeka Njau, are read all over the world. Ngugi believed that African writers should write in their own languages rather in than colonial languages such as English. In 1980 he published the first modern novel in the Gikuyu language.

Art to Use or Wear

Kenya has many artistic styles, but most of them share one thing in common: They are intended to be used or worn, not just looked at. They include the decorated wooden headrests used by northern herders and the carved wooden doors and chairs of the Swahili.

Women often wear colorful jewelry, including bracelets, headdresses, large necklaces, and belts. Some pieces are made for special occasions such as a wedding or an initiation ceremony. A woman's jewelry reflects her

◀ Woodcarvings of Kenya's wildlife are popular with tourists. Wood carving only became a craft in Kenya after World War I (1914–18); today about 60,000 people earn a living from selling their work to tourists.

▼ The Samburu combine thousands of tiny beads with leatherwork to form intricate jewelry.

wealth and stage of life—whether she is single or married, childless, or a mother of sons.

Some art forms are popular with tourists. The Kisii raise money selling their soapstone carvings of animals and people. The Mijikenda mark the graves of their ancestors with carved wooden poles—but many of the poles have been stolen to sell to collectors.

Artists are adapting Kenyan traditions using modern materials and imagery. Many artists exhibit their work at Paa ya Paa (Swahili for "the antelope rises"), a Nairobi gallery founded by East Africa's best-known artist, Elimo Njau.

A New Nation

ALTHOUGH MANY older Kenyans cannot read, they still have a say in how the country is run. In 2005 all Kenyans got the chance to vote for or against a new constitution. It was an important vote, because a constitution determines how people are governed and how they live with each other. The first constitution had been drawn up when Kenya became independent in 1963. Many people thought it was out of date. So that people who could not read would be able to vote, the symbol for a "yes" vote was a banana. To make a "no" vote, the symbol was an orange. In the vote, more Kenyans chose oranges than bananas and rejected the constitution. It was probably because they were unhappy with the government, which supported the new constitution.

◀ "Yes" supporters at a rally in Nairobi a few days before Kenyans went to the polls to vote on a new constitution.

PROVINCES AND PRESIDENTS

Kenya is divided into about 70 districts. The districts join to form seven provinces and Nairobi area. Central and Western provinces have most of Kenya's farmland. Eastern and North Eastern provinces contain dusty plains but relatively few people. Nairobi area has more people than any one of the provinces.

Every district has a capital with its own town council. Many local officials are elected, but the head of each district is an official chosen by the president. The constitution of 1963 gives a lot of power to the president. Kenyans want to change this.

▶ Demonstrators show their support for the new constitution. When 57 percent of the voters rejected it, the government promised to consult the people and try again.

Trading Partners

Kenya trades with nations all over the world, especially the United States, the United Kingdom, and other African and Indian Ocean countries. Cash crops, fish, and cement are the main exports. Because they are grown to be sold, crops such as tea, coffee, and cut flowers are called cash crops. Kenya's key imports are machinery, crude petroleum, motor vehicles, iron, steel, and plastics.

Country	Percentage Kenya Exports
Uganda	14.0%
United Kingdom	10.4%
United States	9.2%
Netherlands	7.8%
All others combined	56.6%

Country	Percentage Kenya Imports
United Arab Emirates	13.0%
United States	10.2%
Saudi Arabia	9.4%
South Africa	8.6%
All others combined	58.8%

34°E   36°E   38°E   40°E   42°E

SUDAN

ETHIOPIA

• Kakuma

Lake Turkana

Mandera •

Moyale •

UGANDA

4°N

2°N

RIFT VALLEY

• Kitale

WESTERN

• Eldoret

⊙ Kakamega

⊙ Wajir

SOMALIA

⊙ Kisumu

Nakuru ⊙

• Meru

EASTERN

NORTH EASTERN

EQUATOR   0°

TEA PLANTATION, page 54

Nyeri ⊙

FISHERMEN, page 55

NYANZA

CENTRAL

Embu ⊙

Garissa •

Ruiru • • Thika

Nairobi •

JOMO KENYATTA BIRTHPLACE, page 52 AND SCHOOL, page 5

⊛ NAIROBI

Kibera •

"YES" RALLY, page 3, 48, 50

2°S

COAST

TANZANIA

BEACH, page 57

SALT LICK LODGE, page 57

Malindi •

Watamu •

Indian Ocean

MAP KEY

⊛ National capital

⊙ Provincial capital

• Other city

4°S

⊙ Mombasa

0   miles   100

0   km   100

34°E   36°E   38°E

Political Map

JOMO KENYATTA

Born Kamau wa Ngengi near Mount Kenya just after British rule began, Jomo Kenyatta led his country to independence. He became interested in politics in the 1920s and later changed his name. In 1947 Kenyatta embarked on a campaign to demand independence from the British. In 1952 he was arrested and imprisoned. Released nine years later, he became prime minister in 1963 and in the following year Kenya's first president. He urged all Kenyans to forget the past and work together to build a new nation. Kenyatta remained in power until his death.

▲ Kenyans called Jomo Kenyatta *mzee*, a Swahili word for a respected elder.

Kenyan Politics Since Independence

After independence, Kenyans had great hopes for the future. Jomo Kenyatta was a popular prime minister and then president for the next 15 years. He brought political stability, economic progress, and educational advances to Kenya, but he also made sure that only his party could hold power. In 1974, he made all other political parties in Kenya illegal.

The next president was Daniel arap Moi. Kenya prospered, but Moi gave government jobs to people from his own ethnic group. If people criticized him, he put them in jail. Eventually, so many Kenyans were unhappy with Moi that he had to allow elections in which many political parties could take part. Moi won in 1992, but in 2002 Mwai Kibaki led an alliance of parties to power.

Kibaki tried to get rid of corruption in the government. His government soon lost much of its popularity, however. The politicians gave themselves large pay raises, which made many Kenyans angry. People also thought that Kibaki's draft of a new constitution did not place strong enough limits on the power of the presidency.

Living off the Land

Although only 7 percent of Kenya is good farmland, 75 percent of Kenyans make their living from the land. Many farmers grow their own food, such as corn, millet, sorghum, cassava, and vegetables. Others grow cash crops to sell at markets. Growing fruit, flowers, and vegetables is one of the fastest-growing sectors of the economy. Kenyan vegetables and flowers are exported around the world. Some farmers work and sell together in cooperatives. They get better prices and can raise more money to invest in business. Large plantations are often owned by foreign companies.

▲ **Avocado is Kenya's leading export fruit.**

HOW THE GOVERNMENT WORKS

Every five years Kenyans vote to elect a president, who can serve only two five-year terms. As head of state and head of government, the president holds a lot of power. He appoints the cabinet, vice president, and high-ranking judges. The cabinet and vice president are members of the National Assembly, most of whom are elected by the people. The National Assembly passes laws.

GOVERNMENT		
EXECUTIVE	**LEGISLATIVE**	**JUDICIARY**
PRESIDENT	**NATIONAL ASSEMBLY—224 MEMBERS**	**COURT OF APPEAL**
VICE PRESIDENT/CABINET		**HIGH COURT**

On the plains and savannas, people keep herds of cattle and goats for milk, meat, and leather. In the past these herders followed the rains. They lived in temporary huts, and moved from site to site with the seasons. Since the 1990s the government has encouraged herders to settle in one place. That makes it much easier to know where they are and to make them pay taxes. Some of the herders still like to keep moving. They worry that, if there is not enough rain, their herds will eat all the grass and trample the soil. When it rains, the soil washes away because there is no grass to hold it together.

About two-thirds of Kenya's fish catch is exported, the remainder provides food and work for people who live near lakes Victoria and Turkana. On the coast big-game fishing attracts tourists to Watamu and Malindi, where they hope to catch huge ocean fish such as marlin or tuna.

▼ **Tea pickers fill their baskets with leaves and buds, which are then dried in huge sheds.**

Trade and Industry

Most Kenyan factories are small. They are based mainly in Nairobi, Mombasa, and Kisumu. Some process food, mill

grain, make beer, or crush sugarcane, for example. Others make goods that Kenyans need, such as furniture, batteries, cloth, and soap. A few larger factories build cars. They put the cars together from imported kits, like life-sized models.

The people who run many businesses are Asian Kenyans. Their ancestors came to Kenya to work as traders when the British built the first railroad, so trade is in their blood.

Exports like cash crops are cheap compared to Kenya's imports. In 2005 Kenya's exports sold for about 3 billion U.S. dollars, but its imports cost more than 5 billion dollars. The government tries to encourage exports and reduce imports, so that more money stays inside Kenya.

▲ Fishermen return from a day's fishing on Lake Victoria. They throw their catch—mostly Nile perch—into the shallow water to be hauled ashore.

AGRICULTURE

The map shows where Kenya's key plantation cash crops are grown. Pyrethrum is an insecticide ingredient and is made from the plants' flowers.

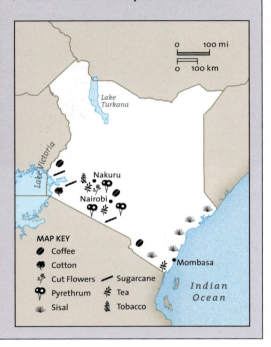

MAP KEY
- Coffee
- Cotton
- Cut Flowers — Sugarcane
- Pyrethrum — Tea
- Sisal — Tobacco

Self-Help Traditions

Kenya's national motto is *harambee*, which means "pull together." By pooling their time and money, people can build schools, clinics, and churches for the whole community.

In towns and cities, people make their own job opportunities. They set up unofficial businesses: All they need is a good idea. They might start a street stall or shine shoes, or collect scrap metal to sell for recycling. There are so many of these informal businesses that they have their own special name: Jua Kali enterprises. The name comes from the Swahili words, *jua*, meaning sun, and *kali*, meaning hot, because many of the workers are outside in the tropical sun. The government is trying to get these traders to become official businesses, so that they pay taxes.

Challenges to Prosperity

Kenya is a place of safety for its neighbors. Refugees often arrive to escape from wars or famine in neighboring Sudan, Ethiopia, and Somalia. It's tough to stop people crossing Kenya's borders. Sometimes, it's hard even to know where the border is! Herders who live near the borders move back and forth across them without any need for a passport.

AIDS is a huge challenge in Kenya, where more than 1.2 million people have the disease. Many children have been left without any parents, and life expectancy is under 50 years. In 2003 the government launched a major offensive against AIDS. More testing, more education, and more treatment seem to have worked. Kenya soon became one of the few countries in Africa where the rate of new infection was falling.

▲ The Salt Lick Lodge is built on stilts around a water hole. Guests can watch the animals that come to drink from their rooms.

▼ The curving white beach at Malindi stretches for four miles (seven km).

Tourism: Kenya's Moneyspinner

Tourism is the second largest earner of foreign money after agriculture. Visitors have always come to see Kenya's wildlife and to relax on its beaches, but some are beginning to explore less visited areas. As local people share more in the profits of tourism, they see the benefits of conserving their environment.

Add a Little Extra to Your Country Report!

If you are assigned to write a report about Kenya, you'll want to include basic information about the country, of course. The Fast Facts chart on page 8 will give you a good start. The rest of the book will give you the details you need to create a full and up-to-date paper or PowerPoint presentation. But what can you do to make your report more fun than anyone else's? If you use your imagination and dig a bit deeper into some of the topics introduced in this book, you're sure to come up with information that will make your report unique!

>Flag

Perhaps you could explain the history of Kenya's flag, and the meanings of its colors and symbols. Go to **www.crwflags.com/fotw/flags** for more information.

>National Anthem

How about downloading Kenya's national anthem, and playing it for your class? At **www.nationalanthems.info** you'll find what you need, including the words to the anthem in Swahili and English, plus sheet music for the anthem. Simply pick "K" and then "Kenya" from the list on the left-hand side of the screen, and you're on your way.

>Time Difference

If you want to understand the time difference between Kenya and where you are, this Web site can help: **www.worldtimeserver.com**. Just pick "Kenya" from the list on the left. If you called Kenya right now, would you wake whomever you are calling from their sleep?

>Currency

Another Web site will convert your money into shillings, the currency used in Kenya. You'll want to know how much money to bring if you're ever lucky enough to travel to Kenya: **www.xe.com/ucc**.

>Weather

Why not check the current weather in Kenya? It's easy—simply go to **www.weather.com** to find out if it's sunny or cloudy, warm or cold in Kenya right this minute! Pick "World" from the headings at the top of the page. Then search for Kenya. Click on any city you like. Be sure to click on the tabs below the weather report for Sunrise/Sunset information, Weather Watch, and Business Travel Outlook, too. Scroll down the page for the 36-hour Forecast and a satellite weather map. Compare your weather to the weather in the Kenyan city you chose. Is this a good season, weather-wise, for a person to travel to Kenya?

>Miscellaneous

Still want more information? Simply go to National Geographic's One-Stop Research site at **http://www.nationalgeographic.com/onestop**. It will help you find maps, photos and art, articles and information, games and features that you can use to jazz up your report.

Glossary

Cash crop a crop, such as tea or coffee, that is grown to be sold.

City-state a self-governing city that rules over the surrounding countryside.

Dialect a regional variation of a language with some words, spellings, and pronunciations that differ from the standard form of the language.

Ecosystem a community of living things and the environment they interact with; an ecosystem includes plants, animals, soil, water, and air.

Endangered a species that is in danger of becoming extinct.

Equator an imaginary line circling the Earth midway between the North and South Poles that divides the Earth into two equal parts.

Extinct a species that has died out.

Fault line a break in the Earth's crust along which movement occurs, causing earthquakes.

Fossil the remains of a plant or animal that lived millions of years ago and has been preserved in some way. In hot, dry conditions whole bones or teeth may survive. In moist locations, buried bones may gradually be replaced with minerals until they become fossilized, or petrified.

Geyser is a hot spring that, from time to time, ejects a column of water and steam into the air.

Glacier a body of ice formed over thousands of years, mainly from layers of snow, that slowly flows on land.

Habitat the environment where an animal or plant lives.

Hominid an early ancestor of modern humans.

Lava molten rock that emerges as a liquid onto the Earth's surface; also the solid rock formed when the liquid cools.

Mangrove a woody tree or shrub with roots that project above the mud, which grows on tropical coasts.

Migration the repeated, usually seasonal, travels of animals (including humans) from one place to another in search of food, better weather, and better conditions in which to raise young.

Plate the outer surface of the Earth is divided into separate panels, like those of a soccer ball, that move constantly. Over millions of years, collisions between the plates form new mountains or troughs in the ocean.

Plateau a large, relatively flat area that rises above the surrounding land.

Rain forest area of dense, broad-leafed evergreen trees and vines that receives at least 80 inches (200cm) of rainfall per year.

Savanna a type of vegetation, consisting of tall grass and scattered trees, that grows in a hot climate with seasonal rain.

Species a type of organism; animals or plants in the same species look similar and can only breed successfully among themselves.

Tropics a geographic region between two imaginary lines drawn around the Earth—the Tropic of Cancer, at 23.5 degrees north of the Equator, and the Tropic of Capricorn, at 23.5 degrees south of the Equator.

Vulnerable a species that is at risk of becoming endangered.

Bibliography

Shaw, Thurston. *Archaeology of Africa*. New York: Routledge, 1995.

Trillo, Richard. *The Rough Guide to Kenya*. New York: Rough Guides, 2002.

http://www.museums.or.ke/ (National Museums of Kenya)

http://www.bluegecko.org/ kenya/ (music)

http://www.kenyaweb.com/ (general)

http://www-sul.stanford.edu/ depts/ssrg/africa/kenya.html (useful links)

Further Information

NATIONAL GEOGRAPHIC Articles

Beckwith, Carol, and Fisher, Angela. "Masai Passage to Manhood." NATIONAL GEOGRAPHIC (September 1999): 52-65.

Caputo, Philip. "Maneless in Tsavo." NATIONAL GEOGRAPHIC (April 2002): 38-53.

Deeble, Mark, and Stone, Victoria. "Kenya's Mzima Spring Comes Alive." NATIONAL GEOGRAPHIC (November 2001): 32-47.

Ehrlich, Anne, and Erlich, Paul. "Kenya: A Population Exploding." NATIONAL GEOGRAPHIC (December 1998): 918-921.

Lambkin, David. "Into Africa." NATIONAL GEOGRAPHIC TRAVELER (October 2003): 106-117.

Lange, Karen. "Meet Kenya Man." NATIONAL GEOGRAPHIC (October 2001): 84-89.

Leakey, Richard. "Serengeti." NATIONAL GEOGRAPHIC TRAVELER (October 1999): 72-76.

Poole, Robert M. "Heartbreak on the Serengeti." NATIONAL GEOGRAPHIC (February 2006): 2-31.

Wainaina, Binyavanga. "Inventing a City: Nairobi." NATIONAL GEOGRAPHIC (September 2005): 36-49.

Zwingle, Erla. "Women and Population." NATIONAL GEOGRAPHIC (October 1998): 36-55.

Web sites to explore

More fast facts about Kenya, from the CIA (Central Intelligence Agency): www.cia.gov/cia/publications/ factbook/geos/ke.html

The Kenya Tourist Board welcomes you with all sorts of information about Kenya: www.magicalkenya.com

Want to know more about Kenya's national parks? Go to the Kenya Wildlife Service (KWS) site, then click the tab for "parks": www.kws.org

Curious abut Wangari Maathai? Learn all about the Greenbelt Movement and the 2004 winner of the Nobel Prize for Peace: www.greenbeltmovement.org

Fascinated by fossils? The Koobi Fora Research Project site provides a field journal continually updated by Louise Leakey: www.kfrp.com

Index

Boldface indicates illustrations.

Agriculture 53
   cash crops 50, 53
   children and **38**
   growing tea **54**
   map 56
AIDS 57
Amboseli National Park 23
   climate 8
Area 8
Ariaal people **28**
Arts and crafts 46–47, **46**, **47**

Bantu speakers 28
Benga music 44
Birds 21
   flamingos 23, **25**
   weaverbirds **21**
Bongos **16**, 21–22
Border 56–57
   nations at the 8
Businesses
   unofficial 56

Carvings
   soapstone **46**
   wood **47**
Cash crops 50, 53
Ceremonies
   initiation 41–42, **42**
Chameleons **25**
Cheetahs 16, **22**
Children **38**, 41
   games 42, **43**
   initiation ceremonies 41–42, **42**
Cities 13, **13**
City-states 32–33
Climate
   rainy seasons 10, 11
Coast 13
   at Malindi **57**
Colonial rule 34–35
Constitution 49, **49**, **50**
Coral reefs 13, **13**
Crops
   cash crops 50, 53

Dance **44**
Districts 50

Ecosystems 16
   map 17
Education and schools 41, **41**
Eid al-Fitr 46
Elephants 16
Elgon, Mount 12
Ethnic groups 37
   Ariaal people **28**
   Gikuyu people 11, 35, 37
   Giriyama people **44**
   Kisii people **46**, 47
   Masai people 37, **37**, 42, **42**
   Mijikenda people 47
   Rendile people **40**
   Samburu people 35, **47**
   Swahili people 32, 44, 45–46
Eunoto festival 42
Exports 50, 55
   avocados **53**
   fish 54

Families **38**, 41
Fishing 54, **54**
Flamingos 23, **25**
Forests
   clearing 21
Fossils 27, 30, **31**

Games
   children's 42, **43**
Gedi
   ruins at **33**
Gikuyu people 11, 35, 37
Giraffes **7**, **15**, 19–20
Giriyama people **44**
Government 53
Great Britain
   colonial rule 34–35
Great Rift Valley **12**, 30
Green Belt Movement (GBM) 24
Groundsel trees 23

Herders 54
   and the border 56–57
   Cushitic 28, **28**
   Nilotic 28

Highlands 8, 10
   wildlife 21–23
Hippopotamuses **22**
Holidays
   national 46
Hominids
   fossils of 27, 30, **30**

Imports 50, 55
Independence 35
   politics since 52–53
Industries 54–55

Jal, Emmanuel **45**
Jewelry 46–47
   Masai **37**
   Samburu **47**
Jua Kali enterprises 56

Kakamega Forest
   wildlife 22
Kemboi, Ezekiel **43**
Kenya, Mount 8, **11**, 12
Kenyan Wildlife Service (KWS) 25
Kenyatta, Jomo 35, **35**, 52, **52**
Kibaki, Mwai 52–53
Kibera (shantytown) 40, **40**
Kimathi, Dedan **34**
Kimeu, Kamoya 27, **27**, **30**
Kisii people
   carvings by **46**, 47
Kisumu (town)
   climate 8

Lake Nakuru National Park 23
Lakes 12
Languages 8, 28, 37
   Sheng (street talk) 45
   Swahili 38
Leakey family **31**
Life expectancy 57
Lions 16, **19**
   man-eating 20
Literacy 45–46
Lowlands
   coastal 11–13

Maathai, Wangari **24**
Magadi, Lake **12**

Malindi (port) 33, 54
  beach **57**
Manda (city-state) 32–33
Mangrove trees 13
Maps
  ancient trading network 32
  climate 8
  Great Rift Valley 12
  historical 29
  hominid finds 31
  physical 9
  political 51
  population 39
  vegetation and ecosystems 17
Masai Mara game reserve
  wildebeests **18**
Masai people 37, **37**
  initiation ceremonies 42, **42**
Mau Mau fighters 35
  Dedan Kimathi and 34
Mijikenda people 47
Moi, Daniel arap 46, 52
Mombasa (city) 13
  carnival 46
  climate 8
  harbor 33, **33**
Monetary units 8
Monkeys
  colobus 22
  vervet **23**
Motto
  national 56
Mountains 8
  Mount Kenya **11**, 12
  vegetation 23
Moyale (town)
  climate 8
Music 44
Mzima Springs 23

Nairobi (city) **13**
  climate 8
  Kibera (shantytown) 40, **40**
  Sheng streek talk 45
National Assembly 53
National parks and reserves 23–24
Ngeneo, Bernard 31
Ngugi wa Thiong'o 46
Njau, Rebeka 46

Pate (city-state) 32–33
Peoples
  early 28
  see also ethnic groups
Phrases
  Swahili 38
Plains 10–11
Plants
  groundsel trees 23
  mangrove trees 13
  see also vegetation
Population 8
  map 39
  rural and urban 38
President 53
Provinces 50

Refugees
  in Kenya 56
Rendile people **40**
Rhinoceroses **20**
Rift Valley see Great Rift Valley
Rivers 8

Safaris 15
Salt Lick Lodge **57**
Samburu people 35
  jewelry **47**
Savannas 7, 10–11
  wildlife 19–20
Self-help traditions 56
Shantytowns
  Kibera 40, **40**
Sheng (language) **45**
Slave trade 33–34
Soapstone **46**
Sport 43, **43**
Storytelling 45
Swahili language 38
Swahili people
  merchants 32
  taarab bands 44
  writers 45–46

Taarab bands 44
Taita Hills
  birds 21
Tea
  growing **54**

Thuku, Harry 35
Tourism 57, **57**
Trade 55
  ancient traders 32–33, **32**
  slave 33–34
  trading partners 50
Tsavo National Park 23
  lions 20
Turkana, Lake **10**
  fossils found near 27, **27**

Vegetation
  mountainside 23
  zones 16, 17
Victoria, Lake **55**
Volcanoes 10, 12

Weaverbirds **21**
"White Highlands"34
Wildlife
  at risk 16, 21
  bongos **16**, 21–22
  chameleons **25**
  cheetahs **22**
  colobus monkeys 22
  elephants **15**, 16
  giraffes **7**, 19–20
  hippopotamuses **22**
  lions **15**, 16, **19**, 20
  protecting 25
  rhinoceroses **20**
  vervet monkeys **23**
  wildebeests **18**
  zebras 19, **19**
Woodcarving **47**
Writers 46

Zebras 19, **19**

Credits

Picture Credits

Front Cover—Spine: Image by © Will Salter/Lonely Planet Images;Top Nigel Pavitt/ John Waburton-Lee Photography; Lo far left: Manoj Shah/Stone/ Getty Images; Lo left: Wendy Stone/Corbis; Lo right: Art Wolfe/The Image Bank/Getty Images; Lo far right: Carl & Ann Purcell/Corbis.

Interior—Corbis: Adria Arbib: 42 up; Yann Arthus Bertrand: 57 up; Bettmann: 34 lo, 35 up; Guillaume Boon: 45 up; Ashley Cooper: 47 up; Werner Forman: 46 lo; Lois Ellen Frank: 53 up; Stephen Frink: 13 up; Martin Harvey; Gallo Images: 18 lo; Gideon Mendel/Action Aid: 38 lo; Thomas Mukoya/Reuters: 3 right, 40 up, 48-49, 50 lo; Michael S. Lewis: 5 up; Carl and Ann Purcell: 47 lo; Jason Reed/Reuters: 43 lo; Radu Sighetti/Reuters: 24 lo; Wendy Stone: 43 up; Torleif Svensson: 40 lo; Liba Taylor: 41 up; Brian A. Vikander: 33 lo, 44 up; Inge Yspeert: 57 lo. Jim Zuckerman: 2 left, 6-7; NG Image Collection: 12 lo; Bruce Dale: 52 lo; Gordon Gahan: 31 lo; Kenneth Garrett: 2-3, 26-27, 30 up; Bobby Haas: 10 lo; Michael Lewis: 11 up, 19 lo; George F. Mobley: 3 left, 36-37, 54 lo, 55up; Michael Nichols: 16 lo; Richard Nowitz: TP; Norbert Rosing: 21 up; Maria Stenzel: 28 up, 41 lo; Medford Taylor: 13 lo, 19 up, 22 lo, 23 lo, 25 lo; Roy Toft: 2 right, 14-15, 20 lo, 22 up, 24-25; Priit Vesilind: 33 up; Superstock: Michele Burgess: 58 up

For more information, please call 1-800-NGS-LINE (647-5463) or write to the following address:

NATIONAL GEOGRAPHIC SOCIETY
1145 17th Street N.W.
Washington, D.C. 20036-4688 U.S.A.

Visit the Society's Web site at www.nationalgeographic.com

Printed in United States of America

Series design by Jim Hiscott.
The body text is set in Avenir; Knockout.
The display text is set in Matrix Script.

Front Cover—Top: A Samburu warrior looks out across the eastern scarp of Africa's Great Rift Valley at Poro, Northern Kenya; Low far left: Two Burchell's zebras nuzzling, Masai Mara National Reserve; Low left: Making a beaded necklace, Rift Valley Province; Low right: Sunset, Amboseli National Park; Low far right: Building in Nairobi

Page 1—A tourist views lions from a safari jeep; Icon image on spine, Contents page, and throughout: Detail of colorful Maasai necklace for sale in a craft shop

09/WOR/1

Produced through the worldwide resources of the National Geographic Society

John M. Fahey, Jr., *President and Chief Executive Officer*; Gilbert M. Grosvenor, *Chairman of the Board*; Nina D. Hoffman, *Executive Vice President, President of Books Publishing Group*

National Geographic Staff for this Book

Nancy Laties Feresten, *Vice President, Editor-in-Chief of Children's Books*
Bea Jackson, *Director of Design and Illustration*
Virginia Koeth, *Project Editor*
David M. Seager, *Art Director*
Lori Epstein, *Illustrations Editor*
Stacy Gold, *Illustrations Research Editor*
Carl Mehler, *Director of Maps*
Priyanka Lamichhane, *Assistant Editor*
R. Gary Colbert, *Production Director*
Lewis R. Bassford, *Production Manager*
Vincent P. Ryan, Maryclare Tracy, *Manufacturing Managers*

Brown Reference Group plc. Staff for this Book

Project Editor: Sally MacEachern
Designer: Dave Allen
Picture Manager: Becky Cox
Maps: Martin Darlinson
Artwork: Darren Awuah
Index: Kay Ollerenshaw
Senior Managing Editor: Tim Cooke
Design Manager: Sarah Williams
Children's Publisher: Anne O'Daly
Editorial Director: Lindsey Lowe

About the Author

BRIDGET GILES studied the geography and religions of Africa at the School of Oriental and African Studies (SOAS), University of London, United Kingdom. Since then, she has written and edited a number of books for children and young adults on the people, cultures, religions, and geography of Africa.

About the Consultants

DR. CHEGE GITHIORA is a lecturer in Swahili at the School of Oriental and African Studies (SOAS), University of London. He specializes in East African languages and the culture of the African Diaspora. Born and raised in Kenya, he makes frequent return trips to the country.

DR. TABITHA OTIENO is professor of social science and Chair of the Social and Cultural Studies department at Jackson State University, United States. Born and raised in Kenya, she received her education degree from Nairobi University. She taught at high school and college in Kenya and was geography supervisor for the Kenya National Examination Council. Her Ph.D. in social science from Ohio University was awarded in 1995.